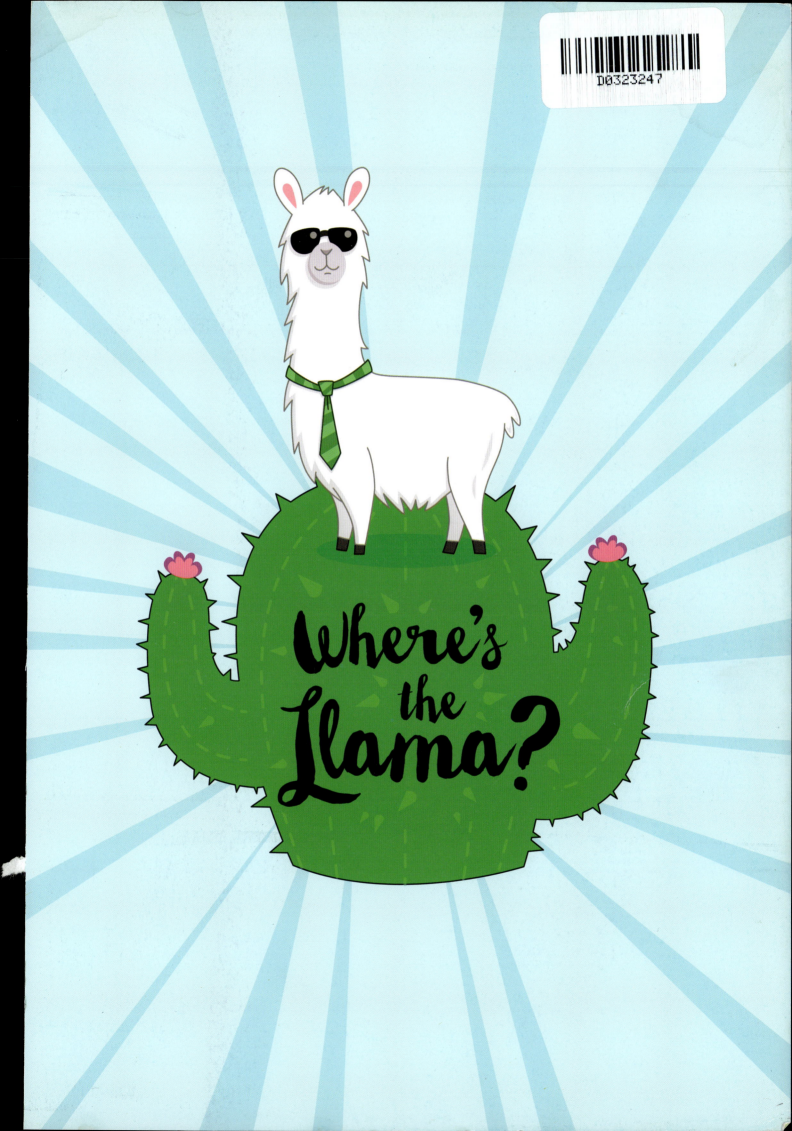

Where's the Llama?

EGMONT

We bring stories to life

First published in Great Britain in 2018 by Red Shed,
an imprint of Egmont UK Limited
The Yellow Building, 1 Nicholas Road, London W11 4AN
www.egmont.co.uk

Text and illustrations copyright © Egmont UK Limited 2018
Illustrated by Artful Doodlers, Tom Connell, Sean Longcroft and Collaborate Agency

ISBN 978 1 4052 9379 2

A CIP catalogue record for this book is available from the British Library.

Stay safe online. Egmont is not responsible for content hosted by third parties.

Egmont takes its responsibility to the planet and its inhabitants very seriously.
We aim to use papers from well-managed forests run by responsible suppliers.

Contents

Introduction

The land where these llamas live may look like paradise, but this herd has itchy hooves! These curious llamas want to trot off to see the world and make some memories they'll never forget, playing hide-and-seek at each and every stopover.

Look out for six llamas and their six cacti friends in each busy scene throughout the book. Be warned though, they're pretty good at hiding. You'll find the answers at the back of the book, along with some extra items to spot.

Let's begin the grand llama world tour!

Meet the Herd!

NO PROBLLAMA

Nothing is a problem for this laid-back llama. He's never in a rush to get anywhere, which sometimes makes travelling as part of a herd a problem! He often pops up in the strangest of hiding places.

SHAMA LLAMA DING DONG

Perfectly preened at all times, Shama loves the limelight, but plays hide-and-seek to win! She laps up the applause if she's last to be found, although her fluffy pink legwarmers often give her away.

LLAMANADE

Llamanade is a homebody at heart and is a little nervous about his herd's globetrotting adventures. He likes his own space, so is rarely found in the thick of things.

DRAMA LLAMA

Drama Llama is the head of the herd, or at least that's what she likes to tell herself. She's great at organising everyone and keeps a detailed travel itinerary hidden under her fleece.

CHARMA LLAMA

Charma by name, charmer by nature! This smooth operator has impeccable manners, greeting everyone he meets with a kind word and a toothy grin. Charma loves travelling to exotic places in search of adventure.

KENDRICK LLAMA

Kendrick is the coolest kid in the flock! He's young, has bags of energy and a certain star quality. He'll happily pose for a selfie with anyone who asks.

Say Hi to the Cacti!

CAL AND CAZ

A pair of prickly pears! Twins Cal and Caz constantly squabble, but don't like to stray too far from one another.

CAMILLA

A kindly cactus, Camilla is often the first to be found in games of hide-and-seek due to her gleeful giggle.

CARLO

Carlo is mad about music and sways in time to the beat whenever the band starts up. Tunes played on panpipes are his absolute favourite!

CASPER

Casper loves to tell anyone who'll listen that he's 167 years young. When he's not fast asleep he's scouting out the best place for his next nap.

CERYS

All-seeing, nothing passes Cerys by – she towers over the other cacti. Truth be told, she's a bit of a gossip.

Bon Voyage!

The llamas have made it down from the mountains and their cacti buddies have hitched a ride too! Now they just have to clear airport security before jetting off for their first adventure!

Kendrick's excitement levels are off the chart, while Llamanade would be glad if he could head straight back home and hit the hay.

Spot all six llamas and six cacti if you can!

Llamas in the Bahamas

The llamas have arrived at their destination – the tropical islands of The Bahamas! Here's where they kick back, relax and soak up some sun. Bliss!

Shama Llama is having a splashing time while No Probllama is hanging out for an ice cream.

Look out for six llamas and their six cacti friends.

Skatepark Search

The llamas may be skating newbies but that won't stop them attempting some insane moves at the local skate park. Llamanade would love to try some scooter stunts – if only he were a little braver! The guys on BMXs are blowing No Problama's mind.

Locate the six llamas and their six cacti buddies.

Movie Night

Lights, Llamas, Action! Our llamas have trotted into town to catch the latest blockbuster movie: *The Alpacalypse 2*. The sweet scent of popcorn was too good to resist for Shama while Kendrick's snack of choice is a giant hot dog.

Find six movie-going llamas and their six spiky friends.

2

Pet Show

Now our herd has hoofed it down to a pet show – if only they had entered! There are cute and cuddly pets, weird and wonderful pets and pets that look like their owners. The llamas go wild for the animal acts on show! Shama has decided she wants a pet poodle, while a goldfish is more Llamanade's speed.

Look out for all six llamas and six spiky cacti.

Winter Wonderland

Brrr! It's chilly out on the mountain, where skiers, snowboarders, tobogganists and llamas are all sharing the slopes. Luckily, our woolly wanderers are never without their coats! Kendrick's too cool for ski school and No Probllama has never felt more chilled!

Spot six wintry llamas and find six cacti too.

A Passion for Fashion

Our dah-lling llamas have headed to Paris for fashion week. Their fur has been styled, their outfits chosen, now they're ready to strike a pose! No Probllama loves his new look and is happily strutting his stuff on the catwalk!

Find six llamas and six cool cacti in the scene.

Football Fever

It's fever pitch at the football stadium as the herd head to see their very first match. Barcellama are taking on Woolly Wanderers in the Chompions League and the teams are ready to go. Wait, what's this? Some llamas are on the pitch! They think it's all edible. . . it is now! Munch!

Spot a team of llamas and a team of cacti. There are six a side!

Las Vegas Wedding

Love is in the air in sunny Las Vegas as another happy couple ties the knot. Llamanade is hoping to see the bride and groom get hitched without a hitch while g-llama-rous Shama Llama is favourite to catch the bride's bouquet.

Locate six lovely llamas and find six cacti friends.

City Carnival

Llamas love to party and the city carnival is the perfect opportunity! There are some truly tremendous sights on display and the herd has met some colourful characters. Join Kendrick, Charma and co as they move their hooves and get into the groove!

Can you spot six partying llamas and six cacti?

Shopping Trip

If there's one thing llamas love to do, it's shop!
No Probllama is checking out some new pyjamas while
Llamanade thinks all the stores are out to fleece him!
He's a glass-hoof-empty kinda llama.

Spot six llamas shopping 'til
they dropand six cacti.

Llamafest

Our lucky llamas have bagged themselves a ticket each for the hottest festival in town – Llamafest! Drama Llama has dug out her wellies while Kendrick Llama takes centre stage.

Look for six dancing llamas and their six prickly cacti friends.

Dancefloor Divas

While the llamas' world tour has been baa-rilliant, the herd is beginning to miss the peace and quiet of mountain life. The flights home are booked, but the llamas can't bow out without one last party. Llama mia, here we go again!

Look for six llamas and their six cacti friends.

Answers

Bon Voyage!

LOTS MORE TO SPOT!

A forgotten teddy bear

Two people fighting over one suitcase

A flamingo inflatable

A pilot's handshake

A happy reunion

A watchful security camera

A lost balloon

A pair of skis

A hopeful hitchhiker

LOTS MORE TO SPOT!

A giant crab

A seagull thief

A metal detector

A sandy ice cream

A scuba diver

A large drinks order

A cool sand creation

An angry lifeguard

A posing muscle man

A banana boat

Llamas in the Bahamas

Skatepark Search

LOTS MORE TO SPOT!

A flat tyre

An enormous pigeon

A bearded man wearing sunglasses

A face on a wall

A backwards boarder

A rocket ice lolly

An awesome granny

A pigeon dance-off

An epic fail

LOTS MORE TO SPOT!

An unusually tall man

A pair of winged 3-D glasses

An autographing actor

A trip hazard

A latecomer

An oversized statuette

A screen number sign

A movie magazine

An alien audience member

A plaited beard

Movie Night

Pet Show

LOTS MORE TO SPOT!

An ostrich rider ⬤
A dog that looks like its owner ⬤
A sunflower with a face ⬤
A cowboy pup ⬤
A skateboarding tortoise ⬤
An acrobatic parrot ⬤
A prize-winning goldfish ⬤
A solitary stick insect ⬤
The pinkest of poodles ⬤
An unfortunate puddle ⬤

LOTS MORE TO SPOT!

A human snowball ⬤
A snowboarding dog ⬤
A mad moose ⬤
An abominable snowman ⬤
A hat with antlers ⬤
A snowman in progress ⬤
Eight helpful huskies ⬤
A sleeping snow angel ⬤
A flying bobsleigh ⬤

Winter Wonderland

A Passion for Fashion!

LOTS MORE TO SPOT!

A sneaky snack

A forgotten hairbrush

A pair of pigeons

A faux fur coat

A backwards baseball cap

A random robot

A chicken costume

A purple cactus

A famous fashion designer

A snowy puppy

LOTS MORE TO SPOT!

An inflatable trophy

A flying boot

A dapper waistcoat

A mischievous mole

A horned helmet

A random rugby ball

A prima donna

A pitch-invading dog

A mega mascot

A team floss

Football Fever

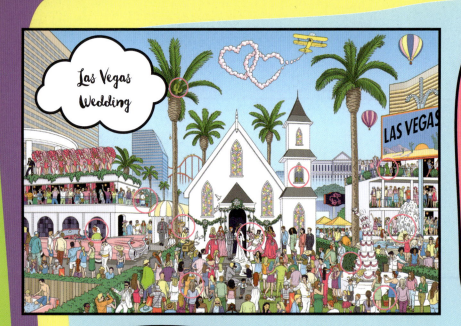

Las Vegas Wedding

LOTS MORE TO SPOT!

- A coconut injury
- Some skyscraper heels
- A magical mermaid
- Some happy hot-tubbers
- An Elvis all in black
- A couple of centurions
- A packed rollercoaster
- A toppling cake topper

LOTS MORE TO SPOT!

- An octopus costume
- A pair of binoculars
- A boy with a tiger face
- A manhole escapee
- A playful pup
- An interesting inflatable
- A hula hoop
- Some helpful litter-pickers
- A colourful fan

City Carnival

Shopping Trip

LOTS MORE TO SPOT!

- A toddler tantrum
- A swirly lollipop
- A pooch in a handbag
- A pink balloon
- A kid on crutches
- A number 7 shirt
- A boy in a bush
- A generous gift-giver

Llamafest

LOTS MORE TO SPOT!

A jolly juggler
A cosy campfire
A pair of portaloos
A barbecue queue
A tambourine dance
A big dog
An acoustic guitar
A treasure chest

LOTS MORE TO SPOT!

Some cola on ice
A pesky paparazzo
Two friends flossing
A woman in a spotty dress
A pair of pink fairy wings
A silver disco ball
A neon disco sign
A pink-haired DJ
A wheelchair raver

Dancefloor Divas